THE UNIQUENESS OF JESUS CHRIST

As Witnessed in the Gospel of John

JIMMY H. DEMOSS

ISBN 979-8-88616-422-0 (paperback)
ISBN 979-8-88616-423-7 (digital)

Christian Faith Publishing
832 Park Avenue
Meadville, PA 16335
www.christianfaithpublishing.com

Unless otherwise stated, scripture quotations are from the New King James Version.

Printed in the United States of America

This book is dedicated to my late and beloved wife of fifty-six years, Lillian (Lil). It was she who encouraged me through the years to write a book on the person and work of the Lord Jesus. It was only after her death that providence afforded me the opportunity to do just that. She was everything a Christian wife should be: her devotion to the Lord in the home, at work, and in His church was exemplary. Her dedication to me and our five children was undivided. To know her was to love her. I am ever thankful to the Lord for His gift of her to me. She would be pleased with the exaltation of our blessed Lord in *The Uniqueness of Jesus Christ*.

Contents

Foreword

The view you have of Jesus Christ is the most important position you will ever hold; in fact, it will determine your eternal destiny. Was He just a man, or was He also God? There is no middle ground. Jesus Himself claimed repeatedly that He was God. And in the words of writer C. S. Lewis, when Jesus made those claims, He was either a *lunatic* (He had lost his mind) or He was a *liar* (He knew that what He was claiming was not true), or He was *Lord* (He was who He claimed to be: God).

My friend Jimmy DeMoss has done us a tremendous favor by proving the latter: *Jesus was (and is) Lord!* Citing thirty references from John's gospel, he demonstrates the absolute uniqueness of Jesus. Any other human being would have to be out of his mind to make the claims that Jesus did. But Jesus was truly a unique person! And in a concluding appendix, Jimmy expands that truth by referring to many other passages from the Gospel of John as to the uniqueness of Christ. If you already believe that Jesus is God and are trusting in Him as your Savior, Jimmy, in a very unusual and helpful way, will help you see the absolute uniqueness of your Savior.

If you have not already come to see that truth, this small book could change your life—for an eternity. You cannot be on the fence about these matters. Whether or not you want to face this truth, someday you will face eternity. And what you think about Jesus Christ will settle your destiny. Was He a mere man? Was He just a good moral teacher? Was He crazy, thinking He was God? Did He lie constantly about who He was? Or was He who He claimed to be—God?

The book you hold in your hands will help you decide. It is brief and to the point, and it will not take you long to get through it. So don't put it away until you have given the absolute uniqueness of Jesus careful consideration.

Curtis Thomas

Acknowledgments

No one person has been as influential in my Christian life as Henry Wood. Henry and I led in the founding of Texarkana Reformed Baptist Church (TRBC) and were the first two pastors/elders of the church, which we pastored together for thirty-five years. He was my pastor, friend, counselor, teacher, brother, and confidant. Our hours spent together as elders—pastoring Christ's church—gave me the privilege of knowing him in all the vicissitudes of the pastoral ministry. He was dependable, wise, knowledgeable, steadfast, focused, humble, and committed to Christ and His church. His urging me to have *The Uniqueness of Jesus Christ* published was the key factor in my moving forward to do so.

Others who helped in various ways (encouraging, proofreading, praying, etc.) are listed here in alphabetical order: Sharon Brower (my oldest daughter), Jimmy H. DeMoss Jr. (my older son), Vollie and Trish Floyd (friends and coworkers in God's kingdom), Nolan Green (a dear friend and Christian brother for over threescore years), Johnny Hinson (my grandson-in-law), Michael Holt (a brother who designed the front cover), Frank McFerrin (a dear brother and confidant for over forty years), Martin Rizley (former copastor and longtime friend, current missionary to Spain), Matt Smart (current pastor of TRBC), Curtis Thomas (longtime friend and counselor), Jerry Watson (my son-in-law), Olive Jane Watson (my great-granddaughter), Susan Watson (my middle daughter), Bobby Wilson (a dear Christian friend), and others whom I have inadvertently missed.

A special thanks to Texarkana Reformed Baptist Church, where I served as pastor/elder for forty years—for their support, their recognition of me as their pastor/overseer, their prayers, and their aid and love given to me in carrying out the overall ministry of TRBC (Hebrews 13:17). Again, *thank you all!*

Jimmy H. DeMoss
October 2022

Introduction

Jesus Christ is the most unique person to ever appear on this earth. He was born to a poor Jewish couple in an obscure little village in the land of Palestine some two thousand years ago. Yet His birth divided history in two parts: "before Christ" (BC) and *anno Domini* ("in the year of the Lord"). His coming had been spoken of for centuries by prophets of God in the Old Testament scriptures. Though there were hope and great expectation of His coming, yet few knew much about Him, and those were in a comparatively small nation that was, at the time of His birth, in subjection to the Roman Empire. However, Paul, one of His apostles, said this in a letter to the churches of Galatia:

> But when the fullness of the time had come,
> God sent forth His Son, born of a woman, born
> under the law, to redeem those who were under
> the law, that we might receive the adoption as
> sons. (Galatians 4:4–5)

His birth was unique. He was born of a virgin. When Mary was told that she would give birth to the Son of the Highest, she asked how this could be since she did not know a man. The angel replied, "The Holy Spirit will come upon you, and the power of the Highest will overshadow you; therefore, also, that Holy One who is to be born will be called the Son of God" (Luke 1:35).

He was known by the New Testament writers as the Messiah (Christ), Emmanuel (God with us), Jesus, Lord, Master, Logos (Word), Son of God, Son of man, Son of David, Rabbi (Teacher), King, Prophet,

Priest, Holy One, and more. It is this incomparable Person that we all need to know, and know personally in order to be right with God.

A couple of years ago, I had back surgery in St. Louis, Missouri. In preparation for the surgery, I spent considerable time in the office of the institute's coordinator. She was kind, compassionate, and very helpful in every way as she guided me through all the preparatory stages of the surgery. While in her office, I commented on two beautiful crystals she had—one on her desk and the other in the window. She stated that some people don't believe they are crystals, and some think that they have some kind of healing properties (or something like that). A short time later, she told me that she was not a "Christ follower." I am not sure what precipitated this statement, but at that time, the subject changed, and I was not able to respond. However, a short time later, I had the opportunity to reply to her statements about the crystals and her not being a Christ follower. I told her that I was a Christ follower, and since He was a special person (namely, the Son of God), He could and did work miracles. I also said that inanimate objects had no power to do anything. Our time together ended, and I was left not believing that I had been able to give her all the information that she needed to know about the Lord Jesus. This was in late October 2017. In God's providence, Christmastime provided the opportunity that I had missed back in October. I sent her a beautiful Christmas card from Joni Tada's collection along with a letter about my recovery progress, my appreciation for all her help while I was in St. Louis, and further information on our discussion about Christ. Below is that portion of the letter:

> As Christmas came around, when there is a special focus on Christ, I thought of your statement when I was in your office. You may remember. You said, "I am not a Christ follower." I am not sure what the occasion was, but I responded a little later that I was a follower of Christ and that I had thought a lot about that brief interchange. My conclusion: "I don't think you have given Him a fair hearing." C. S. Lewis

stated that Jesus was either a "lunatic, liar, or the Lord" [taken from *Mere Christianity*, p. 45, The Christian Library Edition]. Although Lewis was once an atheist, he came to believe that Jesus was who He said He was: the Son of God.

Rosetta [name changed to protect her privacy], may I suggest that you give Christ a fair hearing by reading the Gospel of John, the fourth book in the New Testament. The apostle John wrote this account of Christ's ministry near the end of the first century. John himself states what he thinks of Jesus throughout the book, but more significantly, he records what Christ says of Himself. *His claims are stupendous.* For example, He claims to be "the Bread of Life," "the Good Shepherd," "the Truth" (John 6:35; 10:11; 14:6). In addition, the miracles that He works confirm that what He claims of Himself is the truth.

Rosetta, please read this account that John gives of Christ. John, who was a companion and eyewitness of Christ's ministry during the final three years of His life, is compelling. May this reading help you to be able to say, "I am a Christ follower."

This interchange with *Rosetta* made me think of the millions of people who do not give Jesus a fair hearing. They are not believers because of their lack of interest, or they don't have time for Christ or for many other reasons. It's as if they never heard of Him. They appear to be like the Athenians to whom the apostle Paul preached in the middle of the first century. They were worshipping, among other things, a large stone they called "The Unknown God." Paul said to them,

> God, who made the world and everything
> in it, since He is Lord of heaven and earth, does

not dwell in temples made with hands. Nor is He worshiped with men's hands, as though He needed anything, since He gives to all life, breath, and all things. And He has made from one blood every nation of men to dwell on all the face of the earth, and has determined their preappointed times and the boundaries of their dwellings, so that they should seek the Lord, in the hope that they might grope for Him and find Him, though He is not far from each one of us; for in Him we live and move and have our being, as also some of your own poets have said, "For we are also His offspring." Therefore, since we are the offspring of God, we ought not to think that the Divine Nature is like gold or silver or stone, something shaped by art and man's devising. Truly, these times of ignorance God overlooked, but now commands all men everywhere to repent, because He has appointed a day on which He will judge the world in righteousness by the Man whom He has ordained. He has given assurance of this to all by raising Him from the dead. (Acts 17:24–31)

In chapter 17 of Matthew's gospel, Jesus took three of His apostles—Peter, James, and John—up on Mount Hermon and was transfigured before them. His face shined like the sun, and His clothes became white as the light. Moses and Elijah also appeared talking with Christ. Peter was so overcome that he said to Jesus,

"Lord, it is good for us to be here; if You wish, let us make here three tabernacles: one for You, one for Moses, and one for Elijah." While he was still speaking, behold, a bright cloud overshadowed them; and suddenly a voice came out of the cloud, saying, "This is My beloved Son, in whom I am well pleased. Hear Him!" (Matthew 17:4–5)

Note that God Himself said, "This is My beloved Son… *Hear Him!*" The Father would have all men everywhere hear His Son. Have you given Jesus a hearing? How much do you know about Jesus Christ? I hope that this little book will be the means for you to hear Him and thus see that He is indeed the incomparable Christ, the impeccable Messiah, the unique Son of God, and the Savior of the World.

This book is based on the Gospel of John, who was an eyewitness of the ministry, the life, the teachings, and the death, burial, resurrection, and ascension of Jesus Christ. I read through this gospel a number of times with the purpose in mind of discovering the many things that indicated that Christ was unique. I was amazed at the many testimonies that declared—directly or indirectly—the uniqueness of Jesus. There were 106. After spending more time in the gospel since then, I am convinced that my count came up short. Be that as it may, I want to share with you thirty of the special things about Jesus Christ in John's gospel, things that make Him unique: without an equal.

(I believe it would be profitable for you to read through the Gospel of John before you go any further in your reading of this book. Having read through John, you would have gained a measure of familiarity with the gospel that would heighten your interest in *The Uniqueness of Jesus Christ,* since you would have been down this road before. This is just a recommendation.)

1

Early Witnesses to the Uniqueness of Jesus Christ (John 1–3)

1. The Word Was God

In the beginning was the Word, and the Word
was with God, and the Word was God.

—John 1:1–2

John begins this gospel by identifying Jesus as the Word. If there is any doubt that Jesus Christ is the Word in this first verse of John's gospel, verse 14 of this chapter will settle the issue: "And the Word became flesh and dwelt among us, and we beheld His glory, the glory as of the only begotten of the Father, full of grace and truth." Jesus is the Word, who, in every way, is God and who shared the heavenly glory with the Father before the creation of the world (John 17:5).

John could know only by divine revelation what he himself states in the first four verses of this book. He, like all the other biblical writers, could know the truth about the nature and attributes of God, the creation of the universe, the origin of man, man's fall into sin, and myriads of other truths beyond human knowledge or reason only by a special revelation from God Himself. As a Christian, I believe that the Bible is the Word of God and the record of Redemptive Revelation that the God of the universe was pleased to give to sinful man so that he could come to know God and be made right with Him. The *1689 Baptist Confession* states the following:

> The Holy Scripture is the only sufficient, certain, and infallible rule of all saving knowledge, faith, and obedience. Although the light of nature, and the works of creation and providence do so far manifest the goodness, wisdom, and power of God, as to leave men inexcusable; yet are they not sufficient to give that knowledge of God and his will which is necessary unto salvation. (*1689 Baptist Confession of Faith*, Chapter I, Paragraph 1)

Note also, the Word was with God, which means there is a distinction between the two, and yet both are equally God. There is only one God. Some say this means that Christ is a lesser god: "a god." But John doesn't say that "he is a god." That would be rank polytheism! John, the author of this book, is a Jew and an apostle to the Jews. If John started off this book by introducing Jesus as "a god," what would the monotheistic Jews think and do when they read this introduction to this most important new book on Jesus Christ, His Person, and His Works? They would no doubt close the book and say "blasphemy."

John says of the Word, "He was God." The doctrine of the Trinity, which was veiled in the Old Testament, is being clearly revealed here in the New Testament. But how could this be? Well, God is inscrutable; what we know about Him and His person is what He is pleased to reveal to us. "To whom then will you liken Me, or to whom shall I be equal?" says the Holy One (Isaiah 40:25). No one can figure Him out. Paul states it like this, "And without controversy great is the mystery of godliness: God was manifested in the flesh" (1 Timothy 3:16).

However, in his very introduction, in the first few verses of this book, John recognizes His Deity. For example: "All things were made through Him, and without Him nothing was made that was made.

In Him was life, and the life was the light of men" (John 1:3–4). What a clear and straightforward declaration this is of the godhood of Jesus Christ. (This passage will be discussed next.)

What does John mean by the "Word"? At the very least, He is the Expression of God, the Truth of God revealed, God's Spokesman to the world, God's Declaration, *the* Prophet of God (John 1:17–18; 14:6–11; 17:17).

Jesus, the Word, is not only God, *but…*

2. The Word (Jesus Christ) Created Everything

All things were made through Him, and without
Him nothing was made that was made.

—John 1:3

This passage declares among other things the eternality of the Lord Jesus Christ. He could not have been a created being since "in the beginning was the Word" and "all things were made through Him, and without Him nothing was made that was made." There was nothing made apart from Jesus Christ; as the Maker of all things, He must Himself be unmade.

The word *was* is very important in this passage. It is used three times in the first two verses. The first time, it declares the preexistence of the Word when things were created. In the beginning, the Word *existed.* When creation began, the Word was; the Word existed. Thus, He is *the only uncreated being* in the entire universe and must precede all created things.

The *uniqueness* of Jesus Christ as Creator of the universe, yes, and everything else that was created is clearly stated here in John. The writer of Hebrews states something comparable to what John says in the first chapter of John. He states that "God made the worlds through His Son" and said to His son, "You, Lord, in the beginning laid the foundation of the earth, and the heavens are the work of Your hands" (Hebrews 1:1–2, 10). (Note also Colossians 1:15–18.)

Jesus not only created everything, *but…*

3. Jesus Is the Light

In Him was life, and the life was the light of men. And the light
shines in the darkness, and the darkness did not comprehend
it. There was a man sent from God, whose name *was* John.
This man came for a witness, to bear witness of the Light,
that all through him might believe. He was not that Light,
but *was sent* to bear witness of that Light. That was the true
Light which gives light to every man coming into the world.

—John 1:4–9

Before we look at Jesus as the Light, a word needs to be said
about the first clause, "In Him was life." Life was in Jesus; life was a
part of His being. He did not obtain life. Life is eternal because Jesus
is eternal. There is the word *was* again. In Him *was* life. He did not,
in some way, obtain it later in His existence. Life and Jesus Christ are
inseparable. You can't have one without the other—another *unique*
thing about Jesus. You and I obtained life at conception, and we will
live as long as God lives: forever. What a sobering thought!

The life of Christ is the means by which men have light. John
the Baptist bore *witness* to Christ by presenting Him to the Jews who
came to see and hear Him preach. Jesus came specifically to give the
light of the gospel to men who are in spiritual darkness so that they
might believe and be saved. Jesus came into this world to fulfill God's
redemptive purpose—to save sinners.

Furthermore, He is the true Light that gives light to every man
coming into the world. Whether it is the light of the natural world,
the universe (John 11:9–10), the intellectual and moral light given
to all men, or the spiritual light given to His own chosen people to
enable them to comprehend spiritual truths, all come from the Lord
Jesus Christ. In His wisdom, when the Lord created man, He created
the eye that gives light to the body so we can see His glorious creation
(Matthew 6:22f; Psalm 19:1–4). Praise to our wise Creator!

Not only does John, the author of this book, speak of Jesus as
the Light, but Jesus speaks of Himself as "the light" (John 3:19–21;

12:35–36, 46), "the light of the world" (John 8:12; 9:5), and "the light of life" (John 8:12).

What a claim by John and especially by Jesus. Is this the claim of a madman, a liar, or the Lord?

He is not only the Light, *but…*

4. Jesus Is the "Only Begotten Son of God"

And the Word became flesh and dwelt among us, and we beheld His glory, the glory as of the only begotten of the Father, full of grace and truth… "And I have seen and testified that this is the Son of God…" Nathanael answered and said to Him, "Rabbi, You are the Son of God! You are the King of Israel!" For God so loved the world that He gave His only begotten Son, that whoever believes in Him should not perish but have everlasting life.

—John 1:14, 34, 49; 3:16

Included in the above are quotes from John the apostle and author of this gospel, John the Baptist, Nathanael, and Jesus Himself. It should be noted that I have also used a passage from the third chapter for emphasis. All believers are called sons of God. But Jesus is unique. He is "the only begotten Son of God." Here we have four witnesses: John, who is writing under the inspiration of the Holy Spirit of God; John the Baptist, who claimed that God revealed to him at the baptism of Jesus that Jesus was the Son of God; Nathanael, who declared that Jesus was the Son of God based on Jesus's knowing things about him that no mere man could know; and Jesus Christ Himself, who testified that He was in this world because of God's love for the world.

Jesus is the most unique being in the universe. There is no one like Jesus Christ. Furthermore, there are many things unique about Christ. He is the second person of the Trinity; He was born of a virgin; He is the God-man; He was a perfect human being; He was sinless; He was God's perfect sacrifice and propitiation for sinners; and much, much more.

There are other things in the passages above that deserve our attention. Jesus is the Word of God, and He became flesh (man). His glory was apparent—He was strikingly different, and He was full of grace and truth. John the Baptist knew Him by the God-given sign of the Spirit descending from heaven and abiding on Him at His baptism. And Jesus, who knew all things, knew the truth about Who He was and why He had come into this world. Does this sound like a lunatic, a liar, or the *Lord* Jesus Christ?

Not only is Jesus the "only begotten Son of God," *but…*

5. Jesus Is "the Son of Man"

> And He said to him, "Most assuredly, I say to you,
> hereafter you shall see heaven open, and the angels of God
> ascending and descending upon the Son of Man."

—John 1:51

> No one has ascended to heaven but He who came down
> from heaven, *that is*, the Son of Man who is in heaven.

—John 3:13

Jesus was what a real man should be! He used "Son of Man" to refer to Himself more than any other designation. In fact, in the four gospels, He used "Son of Man" well over eighty times. It appears that the Lord took pleasure in His humanity, in being a part of His own creation, in being able to submit, as a man, to the Heavenly Father. In no other way could He be made like His brethren and become a perfect substitute in order to save them from their sins (Hebrews 2:5–18). He told Mary Magdalene shortly after His resurrection, "[Go] to My brethren and say to them, 'I am ascending to My Father and your Father, and to My God and your God'" (John 20:17b).

Before moving to the other chapters in John's gospel, please pause and think on the things that you have read about the Word. He was with God and was God. Life was found in Him. He is the

Light. He was the Creator of all things. He became a man (flesh). He was the only begotten of the Father; grace and truth came from Him. He declared (revealed, showed forth) the Father. He was the Lamb of God, the Son of God, and the Son of Man. He was Rabbi, King of Israel, and Messiah. He was omniscient, authoritative, and in touch with heaven. Nathaniel said to Him, "Rabbi, You are the Son of God! You are the King of Israel!" (John 1:49b).

What an introduction we have to the Word of God, Jesus Christ, the Son of God! Did you notice what John (the writer of this letter), John the Baptist, Andrew, Philip, and Nathaniel said of Jesus of Nazareth? All recognized His *uniqueness*! A quote from John the Baptist is typical of *all* their assertions. He represents all the others concerning the uniqueness of Jesus Christ. He said, *"And I have seen and testify that this is the Son of God"* (John 1:34).

Jesus told Thomas—who would not believe the testimony of the other apostles—after His resurrection, "Thomas, because you have seen Me, you have believed. Blessed are those who have not seen and yet have believed" (John 20:19). We are the ones who have not seen, and yet there are many reliable witnesses in this book and throughout the Bible who testify to that great truth of Holy Scripture: Jesus is the Christ, the Son of God, the Savior of sinners. And many of us have been convinced and do believe in Jesus Christ. On the basis of what is written in John's gospel, you will be able to give this glorious person, Jesus Christ, a suitable hearing. And, hopefully, you will also believe.

Jesus is not only the "Son of Man," *but…*

6. Jesus Turns Water into Wine

On the third day, there was a wedding in Cana of Galilee, and the mother of Jesus was there. Now both Jesus and His disciples were invited to the wedding. And when they ran out of wine, the mother of Jesus said to Him, "They have no wine." Jesus said to her, "Woman, what does your concern have to do with Me? My hour has not yet come." His mother said to the servants, "Whatever He says to you, do *it*." Now there were set there six waterpots of stone, according to the manner of purification of the Jews, containing twenty or thirty gallons apiece. Jesus said to them, "Fill the waterpots with water." And they filled them up to the brim. And He said to them, "Draw *some* out now, and take *it* to the master of the feast." And they took *it*. When the master of the feast had tasted the water that was made wine, and did not know where it came from (but the servants who had drawn the water knew), the master of the feast called the bridegroom. And he said to him, "Every man at the beginning sets out the good wine, and when the *guests* have well drunk, then the inferior. You have kept the good wine until now!" This beginning of signs Jesus did in Cana of Galilee, and manifested His glory; and His disciples believed in Him.

—John 2:1–11

I realize this is a rather long quote, but to get the whole context, it was necessary. Besides, this was the first miracle performed by Jesus. In his book *New Testament Survey* (p. 190), Merrill C. Tenney lists seven miracles in the gospel of John and calls them signs because they illustrate the different areas of Christ's power and are "viewed as proof of divine authority and majesty." They are as follows:

Changing Water into Wine	2:1–11	Quality (Time and Substance)
Healing the Nobleman's Son	4:46–54	Space
Healing the Impotent Man	5:1–9	Time
Feeding the Five Thousand	6:1–14	Quantity
Walking on Water	6:16–21	Natural Law
Healing the Blind Man	9:1–12	Misfortune
Raising Lazarus from the Grave	11:1–46	Death

An example of "Time" is shown by the fact that the man who could not walk was made well instantly. This was clearly a miraculous sign.

Not only does Jesus turn water into wine, *but…*

7. Jesus Predicts Raising Himself from the Dead

Jesus answered and said to them, "Destroy this temple, and in three days, I will raise it up." Then the Jews said, "It has taken forty-six years to build this temple, and will You raise it up in three days?" But He was speaking of the temple of His body.

—John 2:19–21

In the context of this passage, Jesus, on His first visit to Jerusalem and the temple, since He began His ministry, encountered merchants selling their wares in the temple courtyard. He turned over their tables and, with a small whip, drove both them and their oxen and sheep out of the temple. "He said to those who sold doves, 'Take these things away! Do not make My Father's house a house of merchandise!'" (John 2:16). The Jews asked Him, "What sign do You show to us, since You do these things?" (John 2:18b). Jesus gave them the sign of the resurrection of His own body. They thought He was talking about the temple at Jerusalem, which had taken forty-six years to build. Had He been so talking, what difference would it make to Him, the Creator of all things in heaven and on earth? (John 1:3). Remember, He is God! He made the heavens and the earth in six days. He could have built the temple simply with the command of His voice. But to raise His own body from the dead in three days is another thing. I'll say it's another thing! But Jesus can and did raise His own body from the dead (John 2:19–22; 20:1–29). This is one of the most compelling statements of Christ's deity in the Bible. He has to be God to raise His own body to life again after being crucified.

On the other hand, this is the most preposterous statement a person could make concerning his death, unless it's true: "Destroy this temple, and in three days, I will raise it up." But remember, this person is unique. He is not just a man; He is God, the Theanthropic Person. Note also John 10:17–18, where Jesus claims the same thing. So here is my question. What do you think of Jesus Christ now? Is He a truth teller or a liar? Is He a sane person or a lunatic? Is He an ordinary man or the Lord of glory?

II

Witnesses to Jesus's Uniqueness During His Public Ministry (John 4–12)

8. Jesus Announces That the Father Has Committed All Judgment to the Son

> For the Father judges no one, but has committed all
> judgment to the Son, that all should honor the Son just
> as they honor the Father. He who does not honor the
> Son does not honor the Father who sent Him.
>
> —John 5:22–23

What an arrogant statement if indeed it is not true: the Son is to be honored as the Father? But it is true as all Jesus's claims are true. And He has the witnesses to verify them. The Lord did not come in His first advent to judge the world, as He states later in this gospel:

> And if anyone hears My words and does not
> believe, I do not judge him; for I did not come
> to judge the world but to save the world. He who
> rejects Me, and does not receive My words, has
> that which judges him—the word that I have

10

spoken will judge him in the last day. (John 12:47–48)

The reason given by Jesus as to why all judgment is given to the Son is that everyone should honor the Son as they honor the Father. Equal honor is to be given to equal persons, thus proving again that Jesus Christ is God. Equal honor is equal praise, equal worship, equal glory, and yes, equal persons. Again, the uniqueness of Jesus shines through.

Jesus came the first time to save the world, but those who reject Him and His message will be judged by Him and His word when He comes the second time. Today He says, "Come to Me, all you who labor and are heavy laden, and I will give you rest" (Matthew 11:28). At the end of this age, He will say to those who reject Him and His word, "I never knew you. Depart from Me, you who practice lawlessness!" (Matthew 7:23b) Today is the day of salvation; tomorrow is the day of judgment.

Not only is Jesus the final judge of all men, *but…*

9. Jesus Claims to Be Able to Bring Life to Those Who Are Spiritually Dead

Most assuredly, I say to you, the hour is coming,
and now is, when the dead will hear the voice of the
Son of God; and those who hear will live.

—John 5:25

Jesus has power in the spiritual realm as He brings new life to the spiritually dead. Other synonymous terms used are the new birth, regeneration, and quickening. In each case, the sinner is acted upon by the power of God, and a new creature is brought forth. His heart is changed, and he is God's son, God's new man (John 3:3–7; Titus 3:5; Ephesians 2:1–2, 4–5).

He not only claims to be able to bring life to the spiritually dead, *but…*

10. At the Last Day, Jesus Will Resurrect All Those Who Are in the Grave

Do not marvel at this; for the hour is coming in which all who
are in the graves will hear His voice and come forth—those
who have done good, to the resurrection of life, and those
who have done evil, to the resurrection of condemnation.

—John 5:28–29

The three most common "omnis" are all in play here. Jesus
must be omniscient, omnipotent, and omnipresent to execute this
incredible task. Just think about what it will take to bring about this
resurrection—the bringing to life all who ever lived on this earth. It's
certainly equal to the creation of the universe. And Jesus said all who
are in the grave will *hear His voice* and come forth. Nothing is more
indicative of Christ's godhood than this unimaginable event.

Not only will He raise all the dead at the last day, *in addition…*

11. Jesus Is the Bread of Life

And Jesus said to them, "I am the bread of life. He who comes
to Me shall never hunger, and he who believes in Me shall
never thirst… Most assuredly, I say to you, he who believes
in Me has everlasting life. I am the bread of life… I am the
living bread which came down from heaven. If anyone eats of
this bread, he will live forever; and the bread that I shall give
is My flesh, which I shall give for the life of the world."

—John 6:35, 47–48, 51

The Lord's use of figurative language is unequaled in His com-
munications and teachings. He is the bread that gives life—eternal
life—to those who partake. Partaking of Christ is interchangeable with
believing in Him. The outcome is the same: eternal life. Throughout
John's gospel, time and time again, we are told that one has eternal

life when he believes in Jesus Christ, the Son of God. What a claim! Who besides Jesus could make such a claim? Throughout history, millions and millions of people have believed His claim and received that promised life. What about you?

Not only is He the Bread of Life, *but…*

12. Jesus Always Pleases God, His Father

And He who sent Me is with Me. The Father has not left Me alone, for I always do those things that please Him.

—John 8:29

No other person could ever say such a thing: "I always do those things that please Him (God the Father)." We (all mankind) are under sin, as Paul declares in his letter to the Roman church: "There is none who does good, no, not one" (Romans 3:12c). Jesus stands alone before the Father in His perfect righteousness. And to have Jesus for our friend is to have His Father as our Father also.

Not only does He always please His Father, *but…*

13. Jesus Claims to Have Existed before Abraham

Before Abraham was, I AM.

—John 8:58

This is a claim to have existed prior to 2000 BC—a claim to be eternal! This is God's everlasting name. It is the name by which He identified Himself to Moses in the burning bush in the desert near Mount Horeb. When God commissioned Moses to go deliver the Israelites from Egyptian bondage, Moses wanted to know how to identify God, the Sender. This is what the Lord said: "And God said to Moses, 'I AM WHO I AM.' And He said, 'Thus you shall say to the children of Israel, 'I AM has sent me to you'" (Exodus 3:14). Jesus is claiming the name that God gave Himself in the Old Testament some 1,400 years earlier. Who could employ this name but God Himself? The Jews understood Jesus when He used "I AM" with reference to Himself. They took up stones to stone Him (John 8:59a) since this was a name of Deity.

Not only has He always existed, *but…*

14. Jesus Is Worshipped

Jesus heard that they had cast him out [*the blind man He had healed*]; and when He had found him, He said to him, "Do you believe in the Son of God?" He answered and said, "Who is He, Lord, that I may believe in Him?" And Jesus said to him, "You have both seen Him and it is He who is talking with you." Then he said, "Lord, I believe!" And he worshiped Him.

—John 9:35–38

It is a clear violation of the Second Commandment to worship anyone or anything other than God Himself (Exodus 20:4). Yet it states of this man who was blind, who was healed by Jesus: "And he worshiped Him." It is the height of sacrilege for anyone to accept the worship that is due to God alone. Note respectively Peter's response to Cornelius and the angel's response to John, who both sought to worship God's messenger:

As Peter was coming in, Cornelius met him and fell down at his feet and worshiped him. But Peter lifted him up, saying, "Stand up. I myself am also a man." (Acts 10:25–26)

Now I, John, saw and heard these things. And when I heard and saw, I fell down to worship before the feet of the angel who showed me these things. Then he said to me, "See that you do not do that. For I am your fellow servant… Worship God." (Revelation 22:8–9) (Note also Revelation 19:10.)

Jesus, on different occasions, accepted worship from others. Who is this person who is worshiped without rebuffing the worshipper? He is the God/man, Jesus Christ, the Almighty, whom the highest angels worship. "And again, when he bringeth in the firstbegotten into the world, he saith, 'And let all the angels of God worship him'" (Hebrews 1:6 KJV). (Fraud? Liar? Lunatic? *No!* I submit to you that He is the Lord of Glory, who alone is to be worshiped.)

Not only is Jesus to be worshiped, *but…*

15. Jesus Is the Good Shepherd

I am the good shepherd. The good shepherd gives
His life for the sheep… I am the good shepherd; and
I know My *sheep*, and am known by My own.

—John 10:11, 14

Chapter 10 in John is one of those beautiful illustrations of Christ's relationship to His people. The security of the sheep is bound up in the love and care of the Good Shepherd, our Lord Jesus Christ. This passage is reminiscent of the beloved Twenty-Third Psalm: "The Lord *is* my shepherd; I shall not want. He maketh me to lie down in green pastures: he leadeth me beside the still waters…" (Psalm 23:1–2 KJV). I remember visiting an elderly lady in the hospital, and I asked her if she would like for me to read the Scriptures to her. She, with gleaming eyes, answered with a hardy yes. I turned to the Twenty-Third Psalm and started to read. She began to quote it herself, and we, in unison, read and quoted the six verses of that beautiful and memorable psalm. Remember, Jesus Christ is the Good Shepherd. He knows His sheep. He leads them. He calls them by their names. He leads them in the right paths. They know Him, and they follow Him, and He gives them everlasting life in heaven with Himself. Are you one of His sheep?

Jesus is not only the Good Shepherd, *but…*

16. Jesus Is the Resurrection and the Life

Jesus said to her, "I am the resurrection and the life. He who believes in Me, though he may die, he shall live. And whoever lives and believes in Me shall never die. Do you believe this?"

—John 11:25–26

This question was asked of Martha at the tomb of her brother, Lazarus. Jesus raised Lazarus from the dead even though he had been dead four days. By this miraculous sign, He demonstrated the truth of His assertion: "I am the resurrection and the life." She believed! Do you? Remember, John—who is writing this biography of Jesus—was an eyewitness of this miracle and the other signs and deeds of Christ that are recorded in this book. He claims to be a truthful witness (John 19:35; 21:24). If what he has written of Christ is not true, then John is a notorious liar, fraud, hoaxer, and deceiver. Nevertheless, he is a brilliant man. How so? In this way: he has conceived such an elaborate and complex hoax that the most celebrated philosophers and scientists in this world could not equal it in ten lifetimes. He has also deceived untold millions of "Christians." However, I believe that John is a truth-teller, inspired by the all-knowing God of the universe to write this glorious account of our blessed Savior and Lord. What a miracle! Nothing is too hard for the Lord.

III

Witnesses to Jesus's Uniqueness in the "Upper Room Discourse" (John 13–17)

17. Jesus Left This World to Prepare a Heavenly Place Where His Disciples Can Be with Him Forever

Let not your heart be troubled; you believe in God, believe also in Me. In My Father's house are many mansions; if *it were* not *so*, I would have told you. I go to prepare a place for you. And if I go and prepare a place for you, I will come again and receive you to Myself; that where I am, *there* you may be also.

—John 14:1–3

One of the most comforting passages in the entirety of the Scriptures is this passage in John 14. It is often a part of funeral services and is designed to comfort those whose Christian loved ones have gone to be with the Lord. Jesus tells this to His apostles shortly after He told them that one of them would betray Him (John 13:18–19, 21), that He would be leaving them and they would not be able to follow at that time (John 13:33–34), and that Peter would deny Him three times that night (John 13:37–38). They, of course, were perplexed and in a state of wonder and grief at all this news. Thus, the Lord's counsel to them was

17

this: "Let not your heart be troubled; you believe in God, believe also in Me." At a time like this, shortly before His crucifixion, Jesus shows His love and concern for His disciples. He says, "Let not your heart be troubled. *You're being taken care of*" (paraphrased). This passage again shows His omniscience—an attribute demonstrating His uniqueness! Jesus is a true know-it-all. He knows all about you and me. Question: Does your knowing this bring comfort or dread to you? If "dread," then trust Him as the Son of God, the Savior of sinners, and you will know Him as your Savior and have that peace that only He can give.

Jesus not only left this world to go prepare a place for His disciples, *but...*

18. Jesus Is the Way, the Truth, and the Life

Jesus said to him, "I am the way, the truth, and the life.
No one comes to the Father except through Me."

—John 14:6

In chapter 1 of John, we noted that Jesus was eternal life. And from His life, light has been given to all men. The way to the Father and His heavenly home has been provided by Jesus Christ alone. There is no other Way to salvation, eternal life, and forgiveness of sins than through Christ. He is also the Truth. Truth originated in and from Christ; there can be no lie in Him. When He speaks, He speaks the truth. This is why the Bible is true: it is given and inspired by God. The Way, the Truth, and the Life are all natural to our Lord Jesus Christ. Sinners throughout the ages have come to Christ by way of the truth found in holy scriptures. And by coming to Christ, they receive God's gift of eternal life.

There is only one way to the Father, and that is through His beloved Son, Jesus Christ. Note, He says "I" am *the* way... Jesus alone is *the* way, *the* truth, and *the* life. We are saved by a person, the living Savior, Jesus Christ. There is but "one Mediator between God and men, the Man Christ Jesus" (1 Timothy 2:5). Also, the definite article precedes each of the words *way, truth,* and *life*—indicating exclusiveness. This is confirmed by the second sentence (clause) in this verse: "No one comes to the Father except through Me." This may seem extreme, narrow, and restrictive. And it is! This is indeed what the Lord means to convey. And since Christianity is the only true religion, there is a great burden on the church to go into all the world and preach the gospel of Jesus Christ to every creature. The Great Commission becomes even more relevant and more essential when we realize that Jesus is the only way to the Father and eternal salvation.

Paul states in Romans 10:15b, "How beautiful are the feet of those who preach the gospel of peace, who bring glad tidings of good things!"

At the dawn of the modern foreign missionary movement, Reginald Heber, in 1819, in the missionary hymn "From Greenland's Icy Mountains," convincingly expresses the necessity of the church's mission to take the gospel of Christ to the far reaches of the world. In stanzas 1 and 3 (*The Broadman Hymnal*, p. 35, 1940), he writes the following:

> From Greenland's icy mountains, from India's
>   coral strand;
> Where Afric's sunny fountains Roll down their
>   golden sand:
> From many an ancient river, From many a palmy
>   plain,
> They call us to deliver Their land from error's
>   chain.
>
> Shall we whose souls are lighted With wisdom
>   from on high,
> Shall we to men benighted The lamp of life deny?
> Salvation! O Salvation! The joyful sound
>   proclaim,
> Till earth's remotest nation Has learned Messiah's
>   name.

Jesus is not only the Way, the Truth, and the Life, *but…*

19. Keeping Christ's Commandments Is, to His Disciples, a Command

If you love me, keep my commandments… He who has
My commandments and keeps them, it is he who loves
Me… If anyone loves Me, he will keep My word."

—John 14:15, 21a, 23a

In the Old Testament, God gave the Ten Commandments to Israel. They all took the form of a command and, for the most part, were prefaced with "Thou shall" or "Thou shall not." In the New Testament, Jesus gives commandments, His word, to His disciples and tells them that keeping them is evidence of their love for Him. Who has the right, other than God Himself, to give people moral commands and expect people to keep them? Jesus must be God. Again, we see the uniqueness of our Lord Jesus. Here's one additional thought. During the Lord's last night with His disciples, He told them this:

> A new commandment I give you, that you love one another; as I have loved you, that you also love one another. By this all will know that you are My disciples, if you have love for one another. (John 13:34–35)

What a challenging commandment to us Christians. The fulfilling of this in our relationship to other Christians is evidence that we love Him who first loved us. Moreover, what a testimony to the world. (Note also 1 John 3:10.)

Keeping Christ's commands is essential *since…*

20. Jesus Is the True Vine

I am the true vine, and My Father is the vinedresser…
Abide in Me, and I in you. As the branch cannot bear fruit

of itself, unless it abides in the vine, neither can you, unless
you abide in Me… for without Me you can do nothing.

—John 15:1, 4, 5c

Jesus is the true vine, and it is only through our union with Him
that we can have spiritual life and produce spiritual fruit, demonstrating our connection to Christ and thus glorifying our Father in
heaven. In this beautiful parable of the vine and the branches, Jesus
shows the absolute need of union between Himself and believers. The
life of the branches depends solely on their vital connection to the
vine. So it is with Jesus and His people. All of the believer's spiritual
life, strength, and productivity depends on being one with Christ.
Both the perseverance and preservation of believers are dependent
on Christ. He said, "Without me, you can do nothing." With the
power and presence of Jesus in our lives, we are overcomers. Without
His help, we are helpless. Without His life, we are lifeless. Without
Him, we are nothing. (Note John 8:31–32.) In short, being vitally
connected to Jesus is all we need!

He is the True Vine, and thus,

21. Jesus Claims Perfect Obedience to His Father

I have kept My Father's commandments and abide in His love.

—John 15:10b

Not one person can claim that he has kept the commandments
of God perfectly. It is impossible for a mere human to be perfectly
obedient to God's law or commandments. This is why we need
Christ's righteousness—because it is perfect. And when it is imputed
to us through faith in Jesus, we are accounted as Christ is: righteous.
Paul states in Romans 10:4, "For Christ is the end of the law for
righteousness to everyone who believes." All who seek to be righteous
by their own "righteousness" fall short of God's requirement for righteousness. But what we could not obtain by a lifetime of works is

granted to us immediately when we believe in the Living Savior, Jesus Christ, who is perfectly righteous.

Jesus is perfectly obedient to His Father, *therefore…*

22. Jesus Promises to Send the Holy Spirit to His Disciples after His Death and Resurrection

These things I have spoken to you while being present with you. But the Helper, the Holy Spirit, whom the Father will send in My name, He will teach you all things, and bring to your remembrance all things that I said to you.

—John 14:25–26

But when the Helper comes, whom I shall send to you from the Father, the Spirit of truth who proceeds from the Father, He will testify of Me. And you also will bear witness, because you have been with Me from the beginning.

—John 15:26–27

I still have many things to say to you, but you cannot bear them now. However, when He, the Spirit of truth, has come, He will guide you into all truth; for He will not speak on His own authority, but whatever He hears He will speak; and He will tell you things to come. He will glorify Me, for He will take of what is Mine and declare it to you.

—John 16:12–14

In chapters 13–17, John records the Lord's most intimate relationship with the apostles, whom He had chosen near the beginning of His ministry some three years earlier. This is known as "the upper room discourse." His public ministry has ended. This last evening with His disciples before His death is special in that it relates a number of significant events: His washing their feet, the announcement of Judas's betrayal of Him (although He does not name Judas), the revelation of His death that was imminent, Peter's denial of Him, His discourse concerning the coming of the Holy Spirit, His relationship to the Holy Spirit, their new relationship with each other and the world, their coming persecution, His advent to the Father, and much more. The last of these five chapters is chapter 17, and it is devoted to Christ's intercessory prayer for His disciples. It is hard to understand the questions, sadness, bewilderment, uncertainties, and other emotions that flooded their minds on this the last night of Christ's life on this earth.

The passages quoted above—from chapters 14, 15, and 16—include the promise of Jesus, after His death and resurrection, that the Father would send the Holy Spirit (Comforter, Helper, Spirit of Truth) in Jesus's name to His disciples. He would bring to their memory what Christ had taught them, lead them into all truth, and "testify of Christ" (John 14:25–26; 15:26–27; 16:12–14). This resulted in the writing of the New Testament scriptures: the infallible written testimony of holy men of God, inspired by the Holy Spirit.

Jesus not only promises to send His Holy Spirit to His disciples, *but...*

23. He Hears His Disciples' Confession of Him as God's Omniscient Messiah the Evening before His Crucifixion

Now we are sure that You know all things... By this
we believe that You came forth from God.

—John 16:30

In this passage, the disciples (apostles) profess the omniscience of Jesus and declare their faith in His having come from heaven. For three years, they had been eyewitnesses of Christ's miraculous signs and had been hearers of His many discourses to both the Jews and the multitudes of His disciples. The evidence was overwhelming and demanded their confession. Having read the above information, can you say with His disciples, "I believe that You came from God, and that You are the Christ, the Son of the living God"?

Shortly after the disciples acknowledge Jesus as the Son of God…

24. Jesus Prays to Be Glorified with the Father

And now, O Father, glorify Me together with Yourself, with the glory which I had with You before the world was… Father, I desire that they also whom You gave Me may be with Me where I am, that they may behold My glory which You have given Me; for You loved Me before the foundation of the world.

—John 17:5, 24

In the light of Isaiah 42:8, Jesus, in this prayer, makes an astonishing claim. He claims to have shared in the glory of the Father in eternity past. Some seven hundred years before Jesus's prayer in John 17, God said, "I am the Lord, that is My name; and My glory I will not give to another, nor My praise to carved images." Again, the incomprehensible doctrine of the Trinity shines through as we compare scripture with scripture.

Moreover, we know that the Father always hears His Son's prayers. As His Son prays at the tomb of Lazarus, He utters the following:

> Father, I thank You that You have heard Me. And I know that You always hear Me, but because of the people who are standing by I said this, that they may believe that You sent Me. (John 11:41c–42)

And just think, Jesus also prayed for us in John 17:20–24. He prayed that we (believers) might be with Him where He is that we might behold His glory. Again, the Father hears His Son's prayers. After my wife died in 2013, I called a dear friend and told her of her death. She exclaimed, "Praise God!" I was, for a moment, taken aback by this. But then I thought, "How wonderful. She is now beholding the Lord's glory."

IV

Witnesses to Jesus's Uniqueness During His Last Days on This Earth (John 18–21)

25. Pilate, the Roman Governor and Judge at Christ's Trial, Told the Jews, "I Find No Fault in Him at All"

Jesus answered, "My kingdom is not of this world. If My kingdom were of this world, My servants would fight, so that I should not be delivered to the Jews; but now My kingdom is not from here." Pilate therefore said to Him, "Are You a king then?" Jesus answered, "You say rightly that I am a king. For this cause I was born, and for this cause I have come into the world, that I should bear witness to the truth. Everyone who is of the truth hears My voice." Pilate said to Him, "What is truth?" And when he had said this, he went out again to the Jews, and said to them, "I find no fault in Him at all."

—John 18:36–38

Pilate's verdict of Jesus is simply "not guilty!" We should see Him the same way, but beyond that, He is righteous, perfectly holy. Not only did He not break God's law, but He kept it perfectly. He died on the cross not for His sins (since He had none), but for the sins of His

26

chosen people. He did something for them that no other creature in heaven or earth could do: He paid for their sins.

Though "not guilty," Jesus was turned over to the Jews, *but…*

26. Jesus Christ Himself Chose Where and When to Die

So when Jesus had received the sour wine, He said, "It is finished!" And bowing His head, He gave up His spirit.

—John 19:30

Jesus gave Himself over to death. Who can know exactly when he will die and then voluntarily release his spirit? No mere human! No one could kill our Lord. The Lord Jesus gave up His life in fulfillment of the Old Testament scriptures and His own prophesy in John 10:

> Therefore My Father loves Me, because I lay down My life that I may take it again. No one takes it from Me, but I lay it down of Myself. I have power to lay it down, and I have power to take it again. This command I have received from My Father (John 10:17–18). (Note also Ecclesiastes 8:8.)

Jesus came to this earth to die for sinners, *and…*

27. All the Miracles That He Executed, Including His Resurrection, Were for the Purpose of Showing That He Was Indeed the Son of God

And truly Jesus did many other signs in the presence of His disciples, which are not written in this book; but these are written that you may believe that Jesus is the Christ, the Son of God, and that believing you may have life in His name.

—John 20:30–31

Jesus did many other signs (miracles) that do not appear in this book (the Gospel of John), but these are recorded for people down through the ages—*for us*—who did not see Him and His mighty works. They are John's own testimony throughout the annals of time, wherever the gospel is preached. And these "are written that you may believe that Jesus is the Christ, the Son of God, and that believing you may have life in His name" (John 20:30–31). Oftentimes, we forget the context in which this statement by John appears. This is one of the many appearances of Jesus to His disciples after His resurrection. Thomas, one of the apostles, was not there. When the others told him about the Lord's appearance, he doubted. Jesus appeared to them a week later. This time, Thomas was there, and as the old saying goes, "seeing is believing." Thomas believed with this exclamation: "My Lord and my God!" Jesus answered him, "Thomas, because you have seen Me, you have believed. Blessed are those who have not seen and yet have believed" (John 20:29). What a reply! Those of us living today—in the early part of the twenty-first century—are not personally privy to those signs. But with the signs and wonders and ministry and teachings of Jesus recorded in the book of John and other New Testament books, many of us were convinced that Jesus Christ, the man from Galilee, is indeed the Son of God and our Savior. Praise His wonderful name!

These signs, culminating in His resurrection from the dead, are proof positive that Jesus is who He said He was—the Christ, the Son of God, the Savior of the world.

Not only did Jesus reveal Himself to His disciples after the resurrection, *but...*

28. Jesus Revealed Himself *Repeatedly* to His Disciples after His Resurrection

This is now the third time Jesus showed Himself to
His disciples after He was raised from the dead.

—John 21:14

The Lord was always concerned about justice and truth. In the Old Testament, before someone could be found guilty of a crime, there had to be, at the least, two witnesses. "One witness shall not rise against a man concerning any iniquity or any sin that he commits; by the mouth of two or three witnesses the matter shall be established" (Deuteronomy 19:15). This was repeated in the New Testament on two occasions: Matthew 18:15–17 and 2 Corinthians 13:1.

In the purpose of God, the resurrected Christ was to be seen numerous times and by many eyewitnesses and groups of eyewitnesses. The Lord appeared at least ten times to hundreds of His disciples after He was resurrected. Records of His appearances are found in all four gospels, in Acts, and in 1 Corinthians. The fifteenth chapter of his letter to the Corinthians is Paul's defense of the resurrection of Jesus. Some of the members of the church at Corinth had been denying the resurrection from the dead. He lists six appearances to demonstrate to those in Corinth that there is a firm foundation for the resurrection of Christ. Each one is preceded by the phrase "that He was seen": thus, they were *eyewitness* accounts. He further argues that if there is no resurrection from the dead, then Christ is not risen, and that leads to false witnesses, empty preaching, vain faith, false hope, and a counterfeit religion. In verse 20, he triumphantly states, "But now Christ is risen from the dead." This fifty-eight-verse chapter is the longest chapter in this letter, and it is all about the resurrection of Christ. It would be good to take a break and read it. It is written by one of the great champions of the Christian faith, Saul (Paul) of Tarsus, an apostle of Jesus Christ and author of thirteen of the New Testament books. Is Paul a liar, a deceiver, a false witness, or a lunatic? I think not!

The resurrection of Christ from the dead is the crowning evidence that Jesus is the Christ, the Son of God, and worthy of all our adoration, praise, and worship. He told His apostles in chapter 15 of John,

> "But when the Helper comes, whom I shall
> send to you from the Father, the Spirit of truth
> who proceeds from the Father, He will testify of

Me. And you also will bear witness, because you have been with Me from the beginning." (John 15:26–27)

Notice that the Holy Spirit will "testify" of Christ, and the apostles will also "bear witness" because they have been with the Lord from the beginning. In other words, the apostles were eyewitnesses of His ministry from the very beginning. The introduction to Acts reiterates this:

> The former account I made, O Theophilus, of all that Jesus began both to do and teach, until the day in which He was taken up, after He through the Holy Spirit had given commandments to the apostles whom He had chosen, *to whom He also presented Himself alive after His suffering by many infallible proofs, being seen by them during forty days and speaking of the things pertaining to the kingdom of God* [emphasis mine]. (Acts 1:1–3)

The forty days after His resurrection and before His ascension to the Father were used to present Himself alive to His Apostles and further instruct them. After His ascension, the 120 disciples chose another apostle to take Judas's place and return a uniform twelve-man witness to the resurrection of Christ.

> Therefore, of these men who have accompanied us all the time that the Lord Jesus went in and out among us, beginning from the baptism of John to that day when He was taken up from us, *one of these must become a witness with us of His resurrection* [emphasis mine]… And they cast their lots, and the lot fell on Matthias. And he was numbered with the eleven apostles. (Acts 1:21–22, 26)

The twelve were all eyewitnesses of the resurrection of Christ, and the resurrection is the crowning evidence that He is the Christ, the Son of God, the Savior of His people (Romans 1:1–4). The evidence is overwhelming. Are you convinced? Do you believe?

Jesus not only died and was raised from the dead, *but…*

29. Jesus Is Sovereign Over All Things

Jesus said to him, "If I will that he remain till I
come, what is that to you? You follow Me."

—John 21:22

Note that the Lord said, "If I will." The Lord's will is sovereign over all things—even hypotheticals. The disciples misunderstood, and some began to pass around the word that John was not going to die. The Lord corrects their failure to include the "if" at the beginning of the instruction to Peter. It is a very important lesson to all of us as well. Don't let the smallest of the teacher's/pastor's words fall to the ground.

> Then this saying went out among the brethren that this disciple would not die. Yet Jesus did not say to him that he would not die, but, "If I will that he remain till I come, what is that to you?" (John 21:23)

In this verse is a lesson for all of us, one with which we started this article: "Hear Him!" We must not only hear Him but we must be careful how we hear (Luke 8:18). Do we hear Him reluctantly and skeptically, or gladly, eagerly, and submissively as Savior and Lord?

The Lord's decrees are established forever in heaven. Nothing can be added and nothing subtracted. We see, time and again, the Lord Jesus exercising His sovereign will through the book of John. For example, in chapter 9, He opened the eyes of a man born blind. This was clearly a miraculous sign, and it was done by Christ so that "the works of God should be revealed in him. I must work the works of Him who sent Me while it is day; the night is coming when no one can work" (John 9:3–4).

We all have a tendency to be occupied with the future. Immediately before Jesus ascended, His disciples asked Him:

> "Lord, will You, at this time, restore the kingdom to Israel?" And He said to them, "It is not for you to know times or seasons which the Father has put in His own authority. But you shall receive power when the Holy Spirit has come upon you; and you shall be witnesses to Me in Jerusalem, and in all Judea and Samaria, and to the end of the earth." (Acts 1:6–8)

C. H. Spurgeon preached a great message over 130 years ago from this passage entitled "Witnessing Better Than Knowing the Future." What a challenging title. Remember, our times are in His hands.

The Lord's life and ministry here on this earth were a busy, eventful, robust, exciting, diversified, thrilling, dramatic, impressive, intriguing, inspiring, exhilarating, and miraculous time. Much, much more could be said, *and...*

30. John Ends His Book by Saying, "This Is Not the End of the Story"

And there are also many other things that Jesus did, which if they were written one by one, I suppose that even the world itself could not contain the books that would be written. Amen.

—John 21:25

This book is just a drop in the bucket of all the words and deeds of the Lord Jesus Christ. Jesus is so great, so wonderful, so industrious, so knowledgeable, so pure, so compassionate, so all-that-is good that the words and deeds coming from so unique a person could not be dictated to a thousand scribes over thousands of years—even if those scribes were using modern-day computers. Because in Him "are hidden all the treasures of wisdom and knowledge" (Colossians 2:3). However, those things that are written in this gospel are sufficient to save the meanest and most depraved sinner who comes to Jesus Christ in faith. We quoted this earlier:

> And truly Jesus did many other signs in the presence of His disciples, which are not written in this book; *but these are written that you may believe that Jesus is the Christ, the Son of God, and that believing you may have life in His name* [emphasis mine]. (John 20:30–31)

Anything that has been written or that is being written is minuscule compared to the subject of John's gospel, the Son of God. The writer of Hebrews—as he summed up the letter he had written—stated, "And I appeal to you, brethren, bear with the word of exhortation, *for I have written to you in few words* [emphasis mine]" (Hebrews 13:22). He had written a rather lengthy letter, and he calls it "few words." Why? Because of the subject. He was writing about the greatness of our Lord Jesus Christ in comparison to the angels, Moses, Joshua, the priests, the sacrifices, and more. What an awesome immeasurable subject!

Amen!

V

Additional Truths about the Uniqueness of Jesus Christ

Extracts from the Four Gospels

1. Jesus rose from the dead. Christianity is the only religion that has an empty tomb (Matthew 28:5–8).
2. Our Lord had an answer for every question (Matthew 22:15–46).
3. His predictions always came true (Matthew 16:21–22).
4. He never lost an argument (Matthew 22:15–46).
5. He knew what others were thinking (John 2:23–25).
6. He had infinite knowledge (John 21:17).
7. He never sinned (John 8:45–46).
8. No one ever spoke like Christ (John 7:32, 45–46).
9. The case for Jesus Christ is flawless (1 Corinthians 15:1–19; Acts 1:1–3). The following are from chapter 5, "The Incomparable Christ," in *Truths That Transform* by D. James Kennedy. Dr Kennedy attributes these aspects of Christ's uniqueness to Dr. Sanders:
    *   "Christ never withdrew or modified any statement He ever made."
    *   "Jesus never once apologized for anything He ever did or said."

34

- "He never sought advice from anyone."
- "He never asked anyone anything."
- "He never once troubled to justify His ambiguous behavior."
- "He never asked for prayer for Himself."
- "He came (into this world) to do something that the founder of no other religion ever did. He came to die—not simply to teach. He came to die for our sins" (pp. 52–54).

Emphasis Placed on *Witnesses* in Scriptures Relevant to the Uniqueness of Jesus Christ

These accounts of John the Baptist, Christ's apostles, and other disciples about what they saw and heard, what they witnessed of the Lord Jesus, are compelling. Either they are telling the truth or they are deranged liars, propagandists, lunatics, and the like. John said at the end of his gospel, "This is the disciple who testifies of these things, and wrote these things; *and we know that his testimony is true* [emphasis mine]" (John 21:24). I think I will take the word of John and the other witnesses of Christ!

Luke the Physician's Account of Witnessing to the Uniqueness of Jesus Christ

Inasmuch as many have taken in hand to set in order a narrative of those things which have been fulfilled among us, just as those who from the beginning *were eyewitnesses and ministers of the word* delivered them to us, it seemed good to me also, *having had perfect understanding of all things from the very first,* to write to you an orderly account, most excellent Theophilus, that you may know *the certainty of those things in which you were instructed* [emphasis mine].

The former account I made, O Theophilus, of all that Jesus began both to do and teach, until the day in which He was taken up, after He through the Holy Spirit had given commandments to the apostles whom He had chosen, to whom *He also presented Himself alive after His suffering by many infallible proofs, being seen by them during forty days and speaking of the things pertaining to the kingdom of God.*

Therefore, when they had come together, they asked Him, saying, "Lord, will You at this time restore the kingdom to Israel?" And He said to them, "It is not for you to know times or seasons which the Father has put in His own authority. But you shall receive power when the Holy Spirit has come upon you; and you shall be *witnesses to Me* in Jerusalem, and in all Judea and Samaria, and to the end of the earth."

"Therefore, of these men who have accompanied us all the time that the Lord Jesus went in and out among us, beginning from the baptism of John to that day when He was taken up from us, one of these must become *a witness with us of His resurrection.*" And they proposed two: Joseph called Barsabas, who was surnamed Justus, and Matthias.

And they cast their lots, and the lot fell on Matthias. And he was numbered with the eleven apostles [emphasis mine]. (Luke 1:1–4; Acts 1:1–3, 6–8, 21–23, 26)

John the Baptist's Account of Witnessing to the Uniqueness of Jesus Christ

There was a man sent from God, whose name *was* John. *This man came for a witness, to bear witness of the Light,* that all through him might believe. *He was not that Light, but was sent to bear witness of that Light.*

John bore witness of Him and cried out, saying, "This was He of whom I said, 'He who comes after me is preferred before me, for He was before me.'" And of His fullness we have all received, and grace for grace. For the law was given through Moses, *but* grace and truth came through Jesus Christ. No one has seen God at any time. The only begotten Son, who is in the bosom of the Father, He has declared Him. Now this is the testimony of John, when the Jews sent priests and Levites from Jerusalem to ask him, "Who are you?" He confessed, and did not deny, but confessed, "I am not the Christ."

The next day, John saw Jesus coming toward him, and said, "Behold! The Lamb of God who takes away the sin of the world! This is He of whom I said, 'After me comes a Man who is preferred before me, for He was before me.'"

And John bore witness, saying, "I saw the Spirit descending from heaven like a dove, and He remained upon Him. I did not know Him, but He who sent me to baptize with water said to me, 'Upon whom you see the Spirit descending, and remaining on Him, this is He who baptizes with the Holy Spirit.' *And I have seen and testified that this is the Son of God* [emphasis mine]." (John 1:6–8, 15–20, 29–30, 32–34) (See also John 3:22–36.)

Paul the Apostle's Account of Witnessing to the Uniqueness of Jesus Christ

Therefore, since we are the offspring of God, we ought not to think that the Divine Nature is like gold or silver or stone, something shaped by art and man's devising. Truly, these times of ignorance God overlooked, but now commands all men everywhere to repent, because He has appointed a day on which He will judge the world in righteousness by the Man whom He has ordained. *He has given assurance of this to all* by raising Him from the dead [emphasis mine].

Paul, a bondservant of Jesus Christ, called *to be* an apostle, separated to the gospel of God which He promised before through His prophets in the Holy Scriptures, concerning His Son Jesus Christ our Lord, who was born of the seed of David according to the flesh, and *declared to be the Son of God* with power according to the Spirit of holiness, *by the resurrection from the dead* [emphasis mine].

Moreover, brethren, I declare to you the gospel which I preached to you, which also you received and in which you stand, by which also you are saved, if you hold fast that word which I preached to you—unless you believed in vain.

For I delivered to you first of all that which I also received: that Christ died for our sins according to the Scriptures, and that He was buried, and that He rose again the third day according to the Scriptures, and that *He was seen* by Cephas, then by the twelve. After that *He was seen* by over five hundred brethren at once, of whom the greater part remain to the present, but some have fallen asleep. After that *He was seen* by James, then by all the apostles. Then last of all *He was seen* by me also, as by one born out of due time [emphasis mine]. (Acts 17:29–31; Romans 1:1–4; 1 Corinthians 15:1–8)

Peter the Apostle's Account of Witnessing to the Uniqueness of Jesus Christ

Simon Peter, a bondservant and apostle of Jesus Christ, to those who have obtained like precious faith with us by the righteousness of our God and Savior Jesus Christ.

For this reason, I will not be negligent *to remind you always of these things*, though you know and are established in the present truth. Yes, I think it is right, as long as I am in this tent, to stir you up *by reminding you*, knowing that shortly I *must* put off my tent, just as our Lord Jesus Christ showed me. Moreover, I will be *careful to ensure that you always have a reminder of these things after my decease*. For we did not follow cunningly devised fables when we made known to you the power and coming of our Lord Jesus Christ, but *were eyewitnesses of His majesty*. For He received from God the Father honor and glory when such a voice came to Him from the Excellent Glory: "This is My beloved Son, in whom I am well pleased." And *we heard this voice* which came from heaven when we were with Him on the holy mountain [emphasis mine]. (2 Peter 1:1, 12–18)

John the Apostle's Account of Witnessing to the Uniqueness of Jesus Christ

That which was from the beginning, which we have heard, which *we have seen with our eyes, which we have looked upon*, and *our hands have handled*, concerning the Word of life—the life was manifested, and we have seen, and bear witness, and declare to you that eternal life which was with the Father and *was manifested to us—that which we have seen and heard we declare to you*, that you also may have fellowship with us; and truly our fellowship is with the Father and with His Son Jesus Christ. And *these things we write* to you that your joy may be full [emphasis mine]. (1 John 1:1–4)

VI

Final Thoughts

As this account of *The Uniqueness of Jesus Christ* draws to a close, I do hope that the purpose has been accomplished: that Jesus has been proved to be the wonderfully unique person that He really is. He was and continues to be unique in every way: He was the glorious Word who left His throne in heaven, and by way of the virgin birth, He became a man like the rest of us—yet "without sin." He lived a perfect life, fully pleasing to His Father. His entire life, with every unique aspect and attribute, was designed to "do whatever God's hand and purpose determined before to be done" (Acts 4:27).

God's purpose was to be glorified in rescuing lost sinners from sin and hell. This must involve the sending of His only begotten Son into the world in the fullness of time to live a perfect life—a life without sin—and die a vicarious death for sinners. Every man is unrighteous and sinful; Jesus was and is both righteous and sinless. Everything we needed to be right with God, Jesus is and has done. Being obedient unto death, He worked out a perfect righteousness that is imputed to all who believe in Him. The gospel preacher or teacher announces the good news (*gospel* means "good news") to lost sinners, exhorting them to repent of their sins and trust Jesus, the Son of God, to save them from their sins. At the very moment one believes in Christ, Christ's righteousness is charged to his account, and he is eternally forgiven of all his sins. God accepts him, clothed in the righteousness of Christ. This righteousness is for all people who come by faith to the Lord Jesus Christ. He is the only way to life eternal. Jesus said, "I am the way, the truth, and the life. No one comes to the Father except through Me" (John 14:6). Hear God's Son. Believe in Him!

Having completely accomplished God's work for Him on this earth, Jesus ascended to the right hand of the Father in heaven, where He is now interceding for His children in this world.

A final word for the reader. *For* those of you who are firm in your Christian faith, I do hope this little book has strengthened your confidence and assurance in Jesus Christ, the Son of God, your Savior. *For* those who profess to be Christians yet lack full confidence and assurance in the gospel, hopefully, this will help confirm and reestablish your faith and confidence in the Lord Jesus Christ and encourage you to hear and follow Him in full assurance that He is indeed your savior. And *for* those of you who are not yet believers, may the eyewitness accounts and words, exhortations, signs, and wonders of Jesus Himself provide the firm biblical foundation for your faith and trust in the living all-powerful Savior of sinners: Jesus Christ, the Son of God.

Everyone must give Jesus Christ a hearing—in this life or in the one to come. Paul, the apostle, said in his letters to the churches of Philippi and Colossae:

> Therefore God also has highly exalted Him and given Him the name which is above every name, that at the name of Jesus every knee should bow, of those in heaven, and of those on earth, and of those under the earth, and *that* every tongue should confess that Jesus Christ *is* Lord, to the glory of God the Father. (Philippians 2:9–11)

> For it pleased the Father that in Him all the fullness should dwell. (Colossians 1:19a)

Appendix

Other Examples of the Uniqueness of Jesus Christ from the Gospel of John

The Gospel of John is the fourth book in the New Testament and one of four gospels. John, the author, was one of the twelve apostles who accompanied Jesus during His three-year ministry on this earth. Having heard Jesus preach and teach, debate the Jewish leaders of His time, and do many miraculous signs, John—being an eyewitness of all that Jesus did and said—is certainly a legitimate witness to us and for Christ. Although John is an eyewitness of Christ, Jesus Himself is His own witness. And my, what a witness He is! But in the Gospel of John, there are many other witnesses who testify for Christ: John the Baptist, the other apostles, the other disciples, the Samaritan woman (John 4:5–42), the officers of the chief priests (7:32, 45–46), the blind man who was healed (9:35–38), and others. Someone has well said that there is no problem with the evidence that Jesus is the Son of God; the problem is with the heart of man who will not believe. Jesus said this to the Jews of His day:

> You search the Scriptures, for in them you think you have eternal life; and these are they which testify of Me. But you are not willing to come to Me that you may have life. (John 5:39–40)

God, in His wisdom, had purposed that from the very beginning of the ministry of Christ, there would be many capable, trustworthy, and believable witnesses to Jesus's ministry as well as His death, burial, and resurrection. Thus, the twelve apostles were chosen early in His ministry to be eyewitnesses of His total ministry: His teaching, His concern and compassion for His own people, His discussions and disputes with religious leaders, and the signs, wonders, and various miracles that He performed. All the above were witnesses to His goodness, greatness, and uniqueness.

The Gospel of John was written for us who were not there to hear and see Jesus in the first century. In this book are the teachings and miracles of Christ, written down and preserved for us that we may come to know Him, believe in Him, and be saved. The Bible is unique in that it is God's special revelation about what He has done to save man from his sins. It reveals the uniqueness of Jesus Christ in prophecy and in person. The first four books of the New Testament are called "gospels." They are about Christ and especially about His ministry on earth: who He was and what He did to save His people from their sins. The word *gospel* itself means "good news." These four books—Matthew, Mark, Luke, and John—are indeed "good news"!

Of all the books in the Bible, John alone provides the greatest amount of information about Jesus Christ, His claims, and demonstrable evidence that He is the only Savior of men. After reading through John many times, I found 106 testimonies from Jesus and others as to His unique identity. As I stated in the introduction, there are probably more testimonies than the 106 I found. But for now, we will settle for the 106. Below are the claims of Christ and His witnesses. There are many names, attributes, characteristics, deeds, signs, and so forth that show the uniqueness of Jesus Christ. They will be kept in order of appearance in the various chapters. Since thirty were discussed in the first part of this book, the remainder will be either listed or briefly discussed. An asterisk (*) at the beginning of the claim indicates it is Jesus Himself who speaks.

The first chapter is rich in descriptions of Jesus, His person, and deeds: His uniqueness. Seven were discussed in chapter 1; the others are shown below.

The Gospel of John

Chapter 1

1. He became man (1:14): "And the Word became flesh and dwelt among us, and we beheld His glory, the glory as of the only begotten of the Father, full of grace and truth." The Word, who was God, became a man in the person of Jesus of Nazareth.
2. Grace and truth come from Him (1:16–17).
3. He is Jesus Christ (1:17). *Jesus* means "savior." *Christ* means "anointed."
4. He is the declarer of God (1:18). See number 1 above.
5. He is the Lord—God Almighty (1:23).
6. He is the Lamb of God who takes away the sin of the world (1:29, 36).
7. He is a Man (1:30). In order to be a perfect sacrifice (a perfect substitute) for sinners, Jesus must Himself be a Man.
8. He is Rabbi (teacher) (1:38, 49). Even the Jewish leaders of Jesus's day realized He was "a teacher come from God" (3:1–2).
9. He is the Messiah (the Christ) (1:41).
10. Jesus knew the disciples before He met them (1:42, 47–48).
11. He is the King of Israel (1:49).
12. *The angels of God minister to Him (1:51). He always has access to heaven.

Chapter 2

13. *He calls the temple "My Father's house" (2:16). He drives out hawkers, vendors, and money changers who were selling animals for sacrifice in the temple courtyard. This is a display of the Lord's reverence for the place of worship.

Chapter 3

14. *Jesus requires a new and spiritual birth of men in order for them to enter the kingdom of heaven (3:3–8).
15. *John 3:16 is perhaps the most well-known verse in the Bible: "For God so loved the world that He gave His only begotten Son, that whoever believes in Him should not perish but have everlasting life." This has been known and loved as one of the most important verses in the entire Bible. Martin Luther called it "the heart of the Bible, the Gospels in miniature."
16. Jesus is above all—another claim of Deity. This time from John the Baptist (3:31).
17. The fullness of the Holy Spirit is given to Christ (3:34). All believers have the Holy Spirit as a gift upon conversion and are exhorted to be filled with the Spirit. But none is full of the Holy Spirit at all times. Only Jesus is!
18. The difference between having eternal life and being under the wrath of God is faith in Jesus Christ (3:36).

Chapter 4

19. Jesus knows all about a woman He just met (4:16–19; 28–29). She had five husbands, and the man she was living with was not her husband. It was this supernatural revelation that made her proclaim, "Sir, I perceive that You are a prophet." And later, she went and said to the men of her town, "Come, see a Man who told me all things that I ever did. Could this be the Christ?"
20. *He claims to be the "Messiah," the Anointed of God (4:25–26).
21. Many of the Samaritans believed that Jesus "is indeed the Christ, the Savior of the world" (4:39–42).

Chapter 5

22. According to the Jews, Jesus called God His Father, making Himself equal to God (5:18).
23. *Jesus calls four witnesses to witness for Him: John the Baptist, His own works (miracles), the Father, and the Old Testament scriptures (Moses) (5:31–40, 45–47). The Father spoke audibly from heaven at Jesus's baptism by John (Mark 1:11) and His transfiguration on the mountain (Matthew 17:5): "This is my beloved Son."

Chapter 6

24. During a storm, Jesus walked on the water (6:16–21).
25. *No one can come to Jesus unless the Father draws him (6:44, 64–65).
26. *Jesus knows the secrets of man's heart. He knew from the beginning that Judas would betray Him (6:64, 70–71).
27. Peter professes that Jesus is the giver of eternal life, He is the Christ, and He is the Son of the living God (6:68–69).

Chapter 7

28. Officers who represent the chief priests and Pharisees confessed, "No man ever spoke like this Man" (7:32, 45–46).
29. No one could interfere with Christ's ministry until the time had come that was predestined by God (7:30; 8:20).

Chapter 8

30. *By the following statement, Jesus dissuades a mob of men from stoning a woman who was caught committing adultery: "He who is without sin among you, let him throw a stone at her first." They all left, one at a time (8:2–12).
31. Jesus claims to be the Light of the World (8:12).

32. *The Father, who sent Christ, bears witness that Jesus tells the truth (8:14–18).
33. *Jesus is sinless (8:46a).

Chapter 9

34. *While Jesus is in the world, He is the Light of the World. He says this in the context of giving sight to a man born blind (9:5).
35. *Jesus claims to be the Son of God (9:35–38).

Chapter 10

36. *Jesus is the sheep's door to eternal life (10:7–9).
37. *Jesus voluntarily lays down His life for the sheep and resurrects it again (10:17–18).
38. *Jesus declares that He is the Christ and appeals to His works (signs) as evidence (10:23–25).
39. *Jesus is one with the Father—one in nature, purpose, power, and authority. The Jews recognized Christ's claim when they picked up stones to stone Him because they accused Him of blasphemy, saying, "Because You, being a Man, make yourself God" (10:30–33).
40. *Again, Jesus claims to be the Son of God, appeals to His mighty works as evidence, and states that the Father is in Him and He in the Father (10:36–38).

Chapter 11

41. Martha professes that Jesus is the "Christ, the Son of God, who is to come into the world" (11:27).
42. *The Father always hears the prayers of the Son (11:41–42).
43. *Jesus raised Lazarus from the dead (11:43–44).
44. His enemies, the chief priests and the Pharisees, said, "What shall we do? For this man works many signs" (11:47).

45. The high priest, Caiaphas, prophesied that "Jesus would die for the nation, and not for that nation only, but also that He would gather together in one the children of God who were scattered abroad" (11:49–52).

Chapter 12

46. The triumphal entry of Jesus into Jerusalem some six days before His crucifixion fulfills the Old Testament prophecies of Psalm 118:25–26 and Zechariah 9:9. He is the King of Israel:

Hosanna!
Blessed is He who comes in the name of the Lord!
The King of Israel [italics mine]! (John 12:13b)

Fear not, daughter of Zion;
Behold, your King is coming,
Sitting on a donkey's colt [italics mine]. (John 12:15)

47. The Pharisees themselves recognized His popularity with the people. They said among themselves, "You see that you are accomplishing nothing. Look, the world has gone after Him!" (12:19)
48. *Jesus knew beforehand that He was going to die by crucifixion (12:32–34).
49. *Jesus again claims that He is the Light among men in the world (12:35–36, 46).

Chapter 13

50. *Jesus knew the very hour He was to depart from this world (13:1).
51. *Jesus is Teacher and Lord to His disciples (13:13–14).
52. *Jesus identifies Judas as His betrayer (13:21, 25–26).

53. *Jesus tells Peter that he will deny Him (13:38).

Chapter 14

54. *To see Jesus is to see the Father (14:7–11). Note also chapter 12:44–50.

Chapter 15

55. *Jesus did works among the Jews that no one else did, which left them without excuse for hating both Him and His Father (15:24–25).

Chapter 16

56. *Jesus claims to have come from the Father to the world. He is leaving the world and returning to the Father (16:28).
57. *Jesus tells His disciples on the eve of His crucifixion that they will all forsake Him and leave Him alone at His death (16:32a).

Chapter 17

58. *Jesus, in His prayer in this chapter, claims that eternal life comes through knowing the Father and Jesus Christ whom He sent (17:3).

Chapter 18

59. The sovereign power of Jesus is demonstrated when the mob came to arrest Him. "He said to them, 'I am He.' They drew back and fell on the ground" (18:6).

60. Peter denied the Lord three times, and immediately, the rooster crowed—in fulfillment of Christ's prophecy in the upper room just hours before:

> Peter said to Him, "Lord, why can I not follow You now? I will lay down my life for Your sake." Jesus answered him, "Will you lay down your life for My sake? Most assuredly, I say to you, the rooster shall not crow till you have denied Me three times." (18:27; 13:37–38)

Chapter 19

61. Pilate defied the Jewish leaders by proclaiming on Jesus's epitaph on the cross, "This Is Jesus of Nazareth, the King of the Jews." And so He was.

Chapter 20

62. *Jesus tells Mary at His tomb to tell His apostles, "I am ascending to My Father and your Father, and to My God and your God" (20:17).
63. The resurrected Christ has a body that goes through closed doors (20:19–20, 26).

Chapter 21

64. After Peter and six others of Christ's disciples fished all night in the Sea of Galilee, they didn't catch one fish. Jesus stood on the bank and told them to cast their net on the right side of the ship. They did and "now they were not able to draw it in because of the multitude of fish" (21:5–6). What a marvelous demonstration of Christ's knowledge of and power over the created order.
65. Peter testifies to the omniscience of Christ: "Lord, You know all things. You know that I love You" (21:17).

66. *Jesus revealed to Peter how Peter would give his life for Jesus when he got old, and in his death, he would glorify God (21:18–19).

Praise for
The Uniqueness of Jesus Christ

My good friend and longtime companion in ministry, Jimmy DeMoss, has devoted his life to searching the Scriptures so as to preach with fidelity the gospel of God—a fact attested to by the well-worn copy of the Bible he keeps on the desk in his study. In this present volume, Jimmy leads us through the Gospel of John as an experienced miner might lead a neophyte through the passageways of a mine, in order to show us how John reveals, in a progressive manner, the unique character of Jesus as the Son of God.

What comes through in this little work is not only the author's high esteem for Scripture—his implicit trust in the divine inspiration and authority of the Bible in all its teachings—but also his love for that incomparable Person whose manifold attributes he delights to show us as he draws forth one golden nugget of truth after another from the pages of the New Testament. The bright sheen of these nuggets, brought together in one volume, sheds light on the divine glory of Him whom all believers rejoice to worship and confess as the Lord of all.

Martin Rizley, missionary to Spain

About the Author

Jimmy H. DeMoss was born and raised in Houston, Texas. Three months after graduating from Milby High at the age of seventeen, he enlisted in the US Marine Corps, where he served three years. In 1956, after being honorably discharged from the Marines, he returned to Houston; and in March of 1957, he married Lillian Gheen, his high school sweetheart. By the end of the year, their first son was born, and Jimmy had himself become a Christian. Three of the most life-changing events in a person's life all happened to him in the space of one year: he got married, his first child was born, and he was converted.

Jimmy enrolled at the University of Houston to pursue a degree in mechanical engineering, but the Lord had other plans. In the fall of 1958, the very night after signing up for three courses in mechanical engineering, he went out to his car in the parking lot of the U of H and began to pray and weep. He had an encounter with God that he has never forgotten. Alone in his car that night, the Lord intervened and stirred up his heart and mind to begin preparing for the gospel ministry. It was a glorious occasion! The next day, he went back to his counselor and changed his major to religion.

In December of 1960, Jimmy; his wife, Lillian; and their two young children moved to Lexington, Kentucky, where he spent the next three and a half years at Lexington Baptist College, where he obtained a BA and ThB. He was also blessed with two new baby daughters. Later, while living in Texarkana, he received a MEd from East Texas State University.

Jimmy has been the pastor of three churches since June of 1964: two in Texas and one in Arkansas. The one in Arkansas—Texarkana Reformed Baptist Church (TRBC) Arkansas/Texas—was constituted by Jimmy and Henry W. Wood Jr. in 1978. He and Henry were also the first two pastors/elders of the church. He retired from the eldership at TRBC after forty years of service. Altogether, he spent fifty-four years in the pastoral ministry. Sadly, after being married fifty-six years, Jimmy's beloved wife, Lillian, died. They have five children, nine grandchildren, and nine great-grandchildren. Jimmy is still an active member of TRBC, where he has been designated elder emeritus. (He also retired from teaching in 1997 after twenty-seven and a half years at Arkansas High School in Texarkana, Arkansas.)